A Temporary Inconvenience

For Joan,

Such a pleasure meeting you.

Andrew

16.06.2012

A Temporary Inconvenience

Andrew Mutandwa

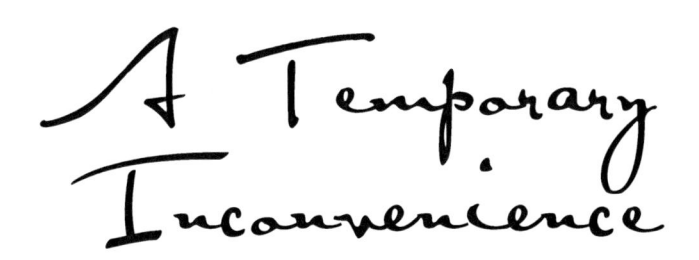

authorHOUSE®

AuthorHouse™
1663 Liberty Drive
Bloomington, IN 47403
www.authorhouse.com
Phone: 1-800-839-8640

© 2011 by Andrew Mutandwa. All rights reserved.

No part of this book may be reproduced, stored in a retrieval system, or transmitted by any means without the written permission of the author.

First published by AuthorHouse   05/27/2011

ISBN: 978-1-4567-8197-2 (sc)
ISBN: 978-1-4567-8196-5 (ebk)

Printed in the United States of America

Any people depicted in stock imagery provided by Thinkstock are models, and such images are being used for illustrative purposes only.
Certain stock imagery © Thinkstock.

This book is printed on acid-free paper.

Because of the dynamic nature of the Internet, any web addresses or links contained in this book may have changed since publication and may no longer be valid. The views expressed in this work are solely those of the author and do not necessarily reflect the views of the publisher, and the publisher hereby disclaims any responsibility for them.

Contents

The prison walls	1
The Faded Picture	2
The making of a one-party-state	3
A slice of pain	6
The happiest Black people	8
In memory of little Rufaro	10
Poor, not very poor	11
Baby in the wardrobe	13
How To Kill A Country	15
In the name of my son	17
The right to dream	19
Crisis—what crisis	20
The Optimist	21
April Fools Coup	22
Slowly, ever so slowly	24
Little claw hammer	25
A to Z in two decades	26
The grim harvest	30
'Till London do us part	32
The privileged	34
The Ambassador	35
The good comrades	36
Intensive Care Needed	37
Post-Traumatic	38
Traumatised	39
The Immigrant Nurse	40

A Mother's Regret	41
The Ugly Truth	42
The Native	43
The Political Lesson	44
The jailing of Nigel 2008	46
Diaspora Grief	47
Epilogue	49
Portrait of a dictatorship	49

Dedicated to the old country and so many broken and unfulfilled dreams. And for every immigrant who has struggled to start afresh and fit in.

The prison walls

The faded prison walls stand cold and uninviting
Seemingly innocent like an old-aged pensioner
Purportedly built for common criminals according to law
But the prison has always harboured one grim secret
Like a serial offender the prison resists rehabilitation

The faded prison walls stand bold and menacing
Apparently guilty like many of the unwilling guests
Supposedly built for the rehabilitation of the offender
But the prison has always punished the political activist
It is a weapon of choice used to silence dissenting voices

The faded prison walls stand burdened by grim secrets
Unwilling to give up tales of the many tortured and killed
Simply for daring to stand up to a dictatorship of the day
But then the prison is only a wife with shifting allegiance
Like a prostitute willing to serve anyone in absolute power

The faded prison walls stand guarding state secret agents
Dubiously extracting confessions from enemies of the state
Inflicting pain in order to gain desperately needed conviction
Victims not knowing whether they will be killed or maimed
Prison walls can be more than a temporary inconvenience

Andrew Mutandwa

The Faded Picture

There is a picture that I carry in my back pocket
There is a picture that I dream about each night
It is a picture from when everything was all right
It is a picture taken when the sun was quite bright
It is not just a picture in my pocket.

There is an image battered and faded from regular view
There is an image of a place that I used to call home
It shows a place I used to know—a place from long ago
It is a place where my father and mother lie buried
It is just a memory I carry around.

There is a picture that I carry in my back pocket
There is a picture that reminds me of a dark night
It is a picture which reminds me it wasn't all right
It is a picture taken when it was all a lie.
It is a memory that haunts my sleep.

There is an image that boldly refuses to fade away
There is an image that reminds me I am so far away
It shows me that where I am can never be home
I am in a place where none of my family where born
It is a place I must now call home.

There is a picture that I carry in my back pocket
There is a picture that is a painting of pain
It is a picture that puts everything in perspective
It is a picture that carries all my memories
Lest I forget that I am an immigrant.

The making of a one-party-state

I was there when he triumphantly rode into town
We were all gathered to give a resounding welcome
Never before had we ever gathered in such numbers
We sang and praised our hero as he basked in glory
He sat there before us and actually appeared humble
Until he stood and punched the air with his fist

I was there on the day they put him on a pedestal
He was the hero his people needed desperately
He talked of reconciliation and the love for his people
He promised free health for all and primary education
That year the harvests were the best in memory
Until he decided the other tribe were all dissidents

I was not there when the Fifth Brigade rode into town
We were all told it was a matter of national security
Never before had a tribe been so intimidated and scared
They said they were here to hunt the dissidents
Everyone was guilty until proven innocent
The President and commander-in-chief had said so

I was not there but everything was kept nice and quiet
State media played its part and told us dissidents were there
Some deaths were reported but they were of dissidents
Armed and ferocious, it was said they roamed the countryside
But always on the run from the majestic Fifth Brigade
Until the Catholics brought out their report

Andrew Mutandwa

I was not there when they dug the sinister secretive mass graves
Villagers watched as families were buried dead or alive
Never before had they ever been forced to celebrate death
They were made to sing and praise the President and his power
Back in the capital he said the war would soon be over
He gloated that the country would soon be a one-party state

I was there when the foreign press challenged the lies
There were reports of mass graves and bodies in old mine shafts
The director of information said it was all lies, damned lies
We were told the Fifth Brigade was a peoples' army
We were reminded the same army had liberated us
But the Catholics had brought out their report

I was there when the painful truth finally came out
What they called choices were simple, sinister and clear
Rape your daughter-in-law in front of everyone or you both die
A village must identify a dissident or everyone will be shot
If a dissident is identified in the village everyone must die
Show enough enthusiasm in praise of the President or die

I was there when the President rode into town
The undisputed leader of a one-party state
Never before had his party been so boisterous
I was there when the Fifth Brigade was paraded
The Commander-in-chief praised a job well done
Flippantly he conceded in war mistakes can be made

I was there when the second revolution ended
Once again the President raised his dreaded fist
The second round of peace had been achieved
He said national unity had now been attained
With him as supreme undisputed leader

I was not there when the other tribe mourned their dead
The dead sacrificed for the goal of socialism
The dead they never got to bury.
Victims of Operation Gukurahundi—Year of the storm

Andrew Mutandwa

A slice of pain

They drag her kicking and screaming
Never mind the infant strapped to her back
Both mother and baby can hardly be seen
Shrouded in the thick silver cloud of teargas
The baby's tiny lungs fight for oxygen
As the huge policeman hovers above

They drag her kicking and screaming
She struggles to protect her crying baby
Both mother and baby are confused
Her skirt is torn and her buttock grazed
The policeman looks on gleefully
As his truncheon aims for exposed flesh

They drag her kicking and screaming
Her screams turn into a tearful whimper
As she tries to reach for the baby on her back
She pleads for her baby to be saved
The riot police look on with amusement
As the blows rain on her buttocks

They drag her kicking and screaming
Relief comes only when she passes out
She is hit one more time just to make sure
Into the back of the police van she is thrown
She lands on her side—on the baby's tiny leg
The policeman shoves her with his big boot

A Temporary Inconvenience

They drug her to stop her from screaming
She has been in hospital for three confused days
An arm is broken and there are head injuries too
And of course the buttocks look massive
She reaches to her side and screams at the empty space
The kind nurse brings her baby to her with a smile

They had drugged her to stop her from screaming
She tries to hug her baby but her hand is broken
She tries the other hand but it is handcuffed to the bed
Salty tears wash her face as she looks at her baby
She had only been queuing for a loaf of bread
There are three other little mouths waiting to be fed.

Andrew Mutandwa

The happiest Black people

In my country things are meant to remain constant
In politics we never change our powerful leaders
There was one long before I could count my fingers
Then came another who said never in a thousand years
He fought a war to keep the others out of power
And told the world his were the happiest Black people

In my country things are meant to remain constant
In politics and everything we only had White leaders
No, we had other leaders, they were headmen and chiefs
We had Black teachers and nurses and union leaders
But ours was a special democracy where we had no vote
And the world was told we were the happiest Black people

In my country things are meant to remain constant
In politics though sometimes change surely does come
The Prime Minister chose some nice Black people
There were some Black people who were not terrorists
Between them they renamed the country Zimbabwe-Rhodesia
And the world was told we were the happiest Black people

In my country things are meant to remain constant
In politics though inevitably change forces its way
The terrorists never gave up and won the war
The Black they feared most became Prime Minister
He surprised all with the olive branches he offered
Now the world knew we were the happiest Black people

In my country things are meant to remain constant
I cast my first democratic vote and it was the last one
In a one-party state you vote for people not policies
We also learnt a brand new phrase called vote-rigging
The Prime Minister became President and stayed forever
And once again we were someone else's happiest people

In my country things are meant to remain constant
In politics though change comes at a painful cost
Opposition leaders sleep always with one eye open
For the secret police come always on dark nights
Quite often the other eye is shut by police buttons
And we are supposed to be the happiest people

In my country things are meant to remain constant
In politics though we found our deathbed
A third of the population are lost to the dreaded AIDS
The other third are roaming the world as asylum seekers
The rest are held hostage in a disintegrating country
And the world thought we were the happiest people.

Andrew Mutandwa

In memory of little Rufaro

She shuffles her tired feet away from the nursing home
The bus comes in an hour but her eyelids are so heavy
She shuffles her tired feet towards home miles away
She passes a charity shop and wearily looks in the window
She thinks of Rufaro the baby she left back home
And wonders if it was worth the trouble

She opens the door to the one room that is her sanctuary
She shares the house with four or seven other people
She never gets to meet them—everyone works all the time
She is tired but she gets on her knees to pray
Her mother always told her to kneel down and pray
She is an asylum seeker, an illegal immigrant

There is a letter from her mother—prices have gone up again
The rains are very late and there are food shortages
Little Rufaro is growing out of her clothes and eats more
The country has no electricity, no water and no money
The Pounds she sent fetched quite a lot on the black market
But in Zimbabwe everyone can do with a little bit more

She reads the letter again very slowly and her heart sinks
Her widowed mother needs her—her daughter needs her too
At work they are making noises about work permits
She says The Lord's Prayer and cries herself to sleep
She dreams of little Rufaro and the lover who abandoned them
She wakes up still tired, worried and ready for another shift.

[Rufaro is a Zimbabwean name which means 'happiness']

Poor, not very poor

When I was growing up we were poor, not very poor
When I was growing up rice and chicken were seasonal treats
When I was growing up we had rice and chicken on Christmas
When I was growing up rice and chicken returned at Easter
When I was growing up we feasted after Good Friday
When I was growing up we then waited for Rhodes and Founders
A holiday mainly for the White folks, but never mind
When I was growing up we could not afford chicken and rice

When I was growing up we were poor, not very poor
When I was growing up we sometimes had tea with bread
When I was growing up sliced bread was not yet invented
When I was growing up we walked miles to buy bread
When I was growing up bread had no best used by
When I was growing up we ate leftovers as long as they were there
When I was growing up it was not always easy to get bread

After I grew up we became less poor, certainly not poor
After I grew up the country seemed awash with chickens
After I grew up every shop seemed required to sell rice
After I grew up I had rice and chicken for lunch at work
After I grew up my wife served rice and chicken twice a week
After I grew up bread became cheaper and came sliced
After I grew up bread was fresh and best used by tomorrow

After I grew up they told me I was the middle class
After I was in middle class I became poor again
After I was in middle class the country had no rice
After I became middle class chicken became a treat again
After I became middle class there was a shortage of bread
After I became middle class I queued for oil, salt and sugar
After I became middle class I was made poor, very poor

Baby in the wardrobe

It all started as a rumour
Tongai said it was sick humour
As he surveyed our pride and joy
A beautiful house in bright yellow
Tongai had toiled long hard hours
Ten years it took buying brick and tile
Another five years for bits and pieces
We scrimped and starved some days
During those difficult building days

It all started as a rumour
Then unravelled the big horror
First came the ruling party youths
They were rough, loud and uncouth
They said the house was unplanned
Never mind the council planning papers
Out came our prized possessions
Dumped like bits and pieces of rubbish
As the bulldozer hovered menacingly

It had all started as a rumour
I wailed as the house fell to its knees
A cheer went up as the youths watched
Like a volcano my anger rose
As the youths bayed like ruthless vicious dogs
I cursed their mothers and their mothers' mothers
I choked on the dust that was once my home
It was then I realised I was not alone
There was a collective communal mourning

Andrew Mutandwa

It had all started as a rumour
But as the sun set not a house was left standing
My kids huddled around the fire scared and confused
Tongai came home a broken dead man walking
He cried like a baby—Tongai cried like a baby
That night the heavens opened as if to settle the dust
I put baby Tinashe in the wardrobe for her to remain dry
As the other little ones huddled under the table
Tongai just sat there, rain mingling with dust and tears

It had all started as a rumour
And it rained every other day for ten days
Baby Tinashe got used to being in the wardrobe
Tongai cried for five days until tears came no more
The President said let's rebuild Zimbabwe together
Now the President was tearing it down brick by brick
When he finally went to sleep, Tongai never woke up
They took away my house, they took away my man

It had all started as a mere rumour
But the President hungered for another revolution
The President said he would clean up the scum
And he gave the world a new phrase
Operation Murambatsvina—Operation Clean-up
The UN asked some difficult questions
The President said all was under control
It has been a hard year and we are still under a tree
Baby Tinashe is now scared of the dark mahogany wardrobe.

[Tongai and Tinashe are Zimbabwean names which mean 'govern' and 'the Lord is with us' respectively]

How To Kill A Country

Take a President always born to be a king
Take a small developing African country
Take a group of dedicated praise singers
That's how to kill a country

Take a President always born to be a king
When Clinton cast an eye on the intern
Americans fought hard to impeach him for lying
That's how not to kill a country

Take a President always born to be a king
With his secretary he has an affair
As the First Lady has renal failure
That's how to kill a country

Take a President always born to be a king
With his secretary he has a child
And tortures journalists who dare to tell
That's how to kill a country

Take a President always born to be a king
Take a President allergic to good governance
Take a President who rigs elections as a hobby
That's how to kill a country

Take a President always born to be a king
Invent a new sport called farm invasion
Take a President who trashes a bread basket
That's how to kill a country

Andrew Mutandwa

Take a President always born to be a king
Take a President who fights foreign wars
While ignoring a raging AIDS pandemic
That's how to kill a country

Take a President always born to be a king
With a government run by his sisters and nephews
Take a country that rewards corruption
That's how to kill a country

Take a President always born to be a king
Take a President who refuses to leave office
Waiting for his son to grow and be crowned king?
That's how to kill a country

Take a President always born to be a king
Take a President who travels in a 20-car motorcade
As his people walk, starve and die
That's how the country was killed.

In the name of my son

Another election and the nation hold its breath
Another election and hope fills many a heart
Another election but democracy it is not

The people queued and voted with determination
They voted and are waiting and waiting and waiting
As fingers are used to count the votes

Another election and even better rigging
In Zimbabwe no one has to be declared winner
In Zimbabwe only the president should win

The people are confused, dazed and angry
They go to their dark homes to wait another term
As they find solace in each other's arms

Nine months from today many babies will be born
A reminder of the freedom that fluttered to deceive
And the memory will be etched in each household

Pity the child conceived this week
As parents are pained by democracy still-born
That child shall be a reminder of dark sinister days

Andrew Mutandwa

One child will be named Rigging Hamadziripi
He will be neighbour to Results Mirirai
Friend to twins Ballotpaper and Ballotbox

Zimbabwean names always have meaning
Witness, Never-mind, No-matter and Exposed
These children are a new message in Zimbabwe.
In the name of my son, Rigged-Again Junior.

The right to dream

I too do have a dream
That one day we will all live in harmony
That my fear of the police will go away
That I will never be tear-gassed again

I too do have a dream
That one day I will have a caring leader
That my president will accept criticism
That I will not be tortured for using my voice

I too do have a dream
That one day I will not be starved because I do not belong
That the right to farm will not depend on the colour of one's skin
That the money in my pocket will have real value

I too do have a dream
That holding elections will not be a declaration of war
That to question government policies will not be treasonous
That being President will not be a job for life

I too do have a dream
That one day I shall be free to roam in Zimbabwe
That never again shall I have to seek asylum
That I shall be free to write again . . .

Crisis—what crisis

Friends, Refugees, Asylum Seekers
Lend me your ears
I come to bury democracy
Never had a chance to praise it
Corruption and dictatorship seem to live forever
While the people's good votes are rigged and lie buried

The noble Mbeki told you there is no crisis
If it's true he was grievously and selfishly uncaring
And grievously shall Zimbabweans answer his call
As the ranks of refugees swell in his backyard
While we flee from a crisis that does not seem to exist
For the noble Mbeki says there is no crisis in Zimbabwe

Here under leave of the African Union and the rest
Come, I, to bury democracy in Zimbabwe
Pan Africanism has become but a dirty word
I stand betrayed by my so-called African brothers
As they warn the world to respect my sovereignty
While I am tortured, jailed and cry out for salvation
But the noble Mbeki says crisis—what crisis?

The Optimist

Beware my people, of those who dismiss your crisis
They refuse to see your pain, sorrow and starvation
Even when you camp on their doorstep begging bowl in hand
Be aware my people—your plight makes them look good.

Arise my people and reclaim your stolen pride and dignity
Return to the days your passport was respected worldwide
Golden days when you were not an object of world pity
Rise up my people so you can hold your heads up again

Speak up my people—against all the cowardly despots
Who group together and seek safety in each other's company
As they hide behind the cloak of so-called Pan-Africanism
Raise your voice my people for silence will still get you killed

Refuse to accept my people, to be held hostage to political mischief
Refuse to accept my people, a tainted inferior form of democracy
Sanctioned by observers severely compromised by political bias
Refuse to accept my people that your vote has to be graded

Stand up my people, to the brutal police and the army bullies
Remind the army and police that they are there to keep the peace
Do not be afraid my people to define what peace means to you
Remain standing my people, in the face of intimidation and torture

Do not lose hope my people—your oppressors are getting old
Face withered and wrinkled the geriatrics shake a bony fist
Shamelessly and proudly laying claim to university degrees in violence
Do not lose hope my people—age is on your side

Andrew Mutandwa

April Fools Coup

There has been a coup in Zimbabwe
The government has toppled the people
The election was an April Fools' Joke
The losers remain defiantly in office

There has been a bloody coup in Zimbabwe
Armed gangs roam the countryside
Death and torture stalk the people
For, they dared to dream of change.

There has been a coup in Zimbabwe
The people have nowhere to run
The people can find no safe haven
As the losers claim their sovereignty

There has been a coup in Zimbabwe
The people are filled with fear
The Chinese send in guns and bullets
As the government rise against the people

There has been a coup in Zimbabwe
The people have a right to be angry
The people look on helplessly
As the world pleads with the strongman

There has been a coup in Zimbabwe
The army and the government close ranks
The police and party gangs give support
As they protect a bunch of cruel geriatrics

There has been a coup in Zimbabwe
Thank God the guns never got delivered
There has been a bloody coup in Zimbabwe
The people feel the loser's brute force

There has been a coup in Zimbabwe
Jails are filled with mothers and babies
As their men groan with broken limbs
An 84-year old grandma is not spared

Slowly, ever so slowly

The election has come and gone
We queued in the morning dew
We queued in the blazing sun
Torture did not break our spirits
The rains did not break the queues

The election has come and gone
The result remain hidden away
Officials pull out the favourite recipe
As they bake and fry the ballots
To serve the president the right result

Little claw hammer

So much power in one scrawny little fist
Shaking in the wind like a plastic claw hammer
Veins snaking all over like dried noodles
The nation trembles in unrelenting fear

So much power in one little scrawny fist
The owner claims university degrees in violence
As his supporters practise for diplomas in aggression
The nation quietly buries their dead

So much power in one little scrawny fist
As the dictator says never, never, never
He defines his idea of what democracy means
As the nation lurches from one day to the next

So much power in one little scrawny fist
Tribalism and racism powers through the withered veins
Fuelling hatred and aggression of the dictator
To punish a people he calls his people

Andrew Mutandwa

A to Z in two decades

A is for the appeal that Zimbabwe's Robert Mugabe enjoyed in 1980
It is also the appeal for salvation that Zimbabweans desperately need
B is for bravery that the war veterans needed to achieve independence
It also now stands for the brutality of their ways to keep Mugabe in power

C is for the change that is needed to bring sanity back to Zimbabwe
It is also for the courage of those who dare to stand up and vote
D is for the deplorable manner in which Africa seems blind to reason
It is also for dictatorship that defines the brotherhood of African leaders

E is for every man, woman and child who has been tortured and killed
It is also for the emigrating millions who seek asylum in far off countries
F is for the little fist of fury that Mugabe shakes to threaten the West and his people
It is also for the new national sport of 'Farm invasion' and Whites bashing

G is for God who seems to have abandoned the ordinary people of Zimbabwe

It is also for the gory images of tortured Zimbabweans hidden from the world

H is for the hatred that Mugabe feels for many Zimbabwean people

It also defines how human rights are a luxury denied to most Zimbabweans

I is for the rampant inflation rate unique to Zimbabwe's ravaged economy

It is also for the international community that does not seem to care

J is for a Judiciary that is so politicised and grotesquely partisan

It is also a tribute to all the brave journalists operating in a hostile environment

K is for the killing fields that the towns and villages of Zimbabwe have become

It also symbolises the kindness of those who said no to Chinese guns and bullets

L is for the lifestyle of the ruling elite who eat cake while the nation starves

It is also for the launderers who have made millions on the thriving black market

Andrew Mutandwa

M is for the people of Matabeleland who were murdered and buried in mass graves
Also dedicated to the many opposition members who have been callously murdered
N is for never, a word favoured by both Ian Smith and Robert Mugabe

Oh if only we had oil, superpowers would have invaded and toppled the regime
O is the outrage of voters denied democracy and tortured for voting the 'wrong' way
P is for the paranoia of Mugabe who sees enemies everywhere he turns
It is also for the abject poverty he has deliberately dragged his people into

Q is for quitting, a word so foreign and meaningless to our power hungry leaders
It is also about the frustrations of President Mbeki's so-called quiet diplomacy
R is how the government has developed expertise in rigging elections
It is also a reminder of how the government refused to release election results

S is for Starving millions ruled by the elite who live in mansions
It also denotes the psychopaths who have helped prop up the regime

T is for threats and terror that characterise all Mugabe's speeches to instil fear

It also stands for the tears that flow in many a household

Unity Accord is how the first opposition was tortured, murdered and subdued

U is also for trade unionists routinely arrested and thrown into dingy cells

V is for the night visits from rampaging and murderous government supporters

It is also the sweet taste of victory when the opposition won an election

W is the warped sense of patriotism by the unprofessional police and army

It is also about a weary, wounded and brutally weakened people

X stands for the stupid xenophobic violence that has claimed so many lives

It is also the need to expose all the atrocities being perpetrated in Zimbabwe

Y is for memory of yesteryear when we had homes, electricity and bread

It is also for the many young people living abroad as illegal immigrants

Z is for the zealots who have betrayed their brothers and sisters

Z is for Zimbabwe which has become another world's disaster area.

Andrew Mutandwa

The grim harvest

The rich brown grass gently sways to a silent orchestra
Basking in the glory of the unforgiving sun of Africa
Unfazed by the searing heat crickets shriek relentlessly
On a thorny bush a laughing dove coos soothingly
It is nature's secret code

He sits in the cool shadows of the thatched farmhouse
The farmer gazes at his fields and plans the harvest
The rains have not been good but the crop is fair
Next season will surely always bring more bounty
It is the farmer's secret wish

The crickets fall silent as if to listen to the rest of nature
The laughing dove flies away in fear of dangers unknown
It starts as a mere whisper but the sounds grow and grow
It is the song that every white farmer fears most
The farm invaders are on the move

They surround the farmhouse and sing songs of threat
The phone line is cut and the road barricaded
The wife desperately suggests they call the police
In the middle of the baying crowd is a bemused constable
It is his duty to protect the invaders

The invaders are the minister's private foot soldiers
The farmer says he will not give up his land and home
He is scared but blind rage gives him courage
He stands guard on his front door as the wife cries
It is defiance that costs him his life

A Temporary Inconvenience

The farmer steps forward to plead with the invaders
Placating and speaking to them in their mother tongue
The invaders feel threatened and a shot rings out
The farmer looks at his killer and knows the battle is lost
It is the last time the farmer will smell the land

The rich brown grass gently sways to a silent orchestra
Basking in the glory of the unforgiving sun of Africa
Unfazed by the searing heat crickets shriek relentlessly
On a thorny bush a laughing dove coos mockingly
It is a month since the farmer died

The minister proudly surveys his new farm and homestead
He and his wife stand on the exact spot the farmer fell
As they gaze at their contraband herd of cattle and fields of wheat
They dream of riches untold and wish for another farm
It is Zimbabwe's theatre of grim harvest

Andrew Mutandwa

Till London do us part

On a hot October night I declared my love for you
I said you were the dream I did not want to awaken from
You rolled your big brown eyes and melted in my arms
You told me you were born to be mother to my children
Nine months and little Tsitsi was born to cement our love

Resplendent in your white uniform you looked so perfect
Never mind that your respected nursing job paid so little
I was a high flying banking executive making good money
We were the toast of all our friends and relatives
Ours was a comfortable middle class life

On a cold June morning I saw Zimbabwe start to change
The election campaign became a declaration of war
There were food shortages and the police became violent
Farmers were chased off the fields in a frenzy of land grab
Nine months and quietly we left for pastures hopefully greener

In London you joined the ranks of the immigrant nurse
No such luck for me the former top Zimbabwean banker
My CV simply added to the growing mound of junk mail
I tried so hard but you said I was being too choosy
Despite the central heating you became colder

Somehow at a nursing home I have ended up a care assistant
When I helped bath an old lady—it just did not seem right
With the shame of my new career my spirit was broken
How I yearn for the days they used to call me Mr so and so
Now I find solace in cheap British beer.

A Temporary Inconvenience

My dear wife worked hard and long hours
She resented me being at home and earning little
I learnt to cook and to do all the house work
Still I was no longer man enough for my loved one
I tried but the temperature kept dropping

My loved one picked up new friends and new habits
Back home they thought we were doing so very well
But she had stopped being the woman I married
She said for me to get real—this is London
And that's when she asked me for a divorce.

[Tsitsi is a Zimbabwean name which means 'mercy']

Andrew Mutandwa

The privileged

They were only playing by the rules
Those honourable members of parliament
Claiming to want to represent me better
If I funded their second home

It was the rules they made themselves
Those honourable members of parliament
Who systematically raided the taxes I paid
As they enjoyed luxury beyond the call of duty

They made such ridiculous rules
Them Westminster members of parliament
They shamed amateurs in developing countries
As they re-defined new boundaries of corruption

Defiantly they defended their rules
Our privileged members of parliament
They needed second homes and duck ponds
To help them attend parliament

They were only playing by their rules
Those honourable members of parliament
Same as in Africa, Asia and South America
We vote so they can be pampered.

The Ambassador

Out of the Benz with a controlled swagger
Overweight but resplendent in a dark suit
They all stand to applaud as he walks in
Filled with self importance he pauses for effect

A trained orator, the ambassador stands to speak
He says disease is ravaging many of his people
The people need food, water and they need shelter
The ambassador begs for millions in more aid

He says his people are going to bed hungry
He blames it all on historical inequalities
It breaks his heart how hungry his people are
But they all look at how big and well fed he is

The donors feel sorry for the ambassador's people
As they get ready to give food, water and shelter
The ambassador then goes and spoils it all
His country wants aid but without conditions.

Andrew Mutandwa

The good comrades

The war of liberation gave me my kind of hero
Straight from the bush with no sense of fashion
Fighters exuding power and sense of compassion
I could believe they went to fight for me

True heroes of the Zimbabwean revolution
They were just so happy to be back home
My heroes were polite and respectful
Their war wounds were a badge of honour

The end of war gave me my kind of hero
There was Hilgard Muller and Gaylord Mao
Nor can I forget comrades Soft, Jinx and Kojak
By 1990 almost all the good ones were dead
True heroes of the Zimbabwean revolution

I miss the true heroes who made me dare to dream
They died happy their own dream had come true
The good comrade died with a dream fulfilled
Never to see yesterday's liberators turn dictators
As the nation now asks, who is a national hero?

Intensive Care Needed

Zimbabwe was a vibrant chubby child
Born to a nation with expectations wild
Promise that belied her troubled pregnancy

As the world embraced its newest member
Violent chequered past remembered no more
A promise that carried hopes of a continent

The desert flower bloomed but for a while
Its genetic disorder lay hidden for sometime
A curse that burdens the so-called dark-continent

Zimbabwe began to cannibalise her children
The cleansing was tribal, political or agricultural
The goal of socialism had to be fulfilled

Zimbabwe was a teenager with co-morbidity
The beautiful child had psychosis and a cancer of greed
A promise now crying out for intensive care

Was there a vaccination that could have helped?
Is there a treatment for this self-harming child?
Or is the promise buried in murder and torture?

Zimbabwe was a vibrant chubby child
Systematically abused by her minders
The shameless rape of a promising future

Andrew Mutandwa

Post-Traumatic

They come for me at three in the morning—always
Never wanted to go to sleep in the first place anyway
I feel that I am losing touch with reality in most ways
I manage to wake gasping for air as I start to drown

They came for me at three in the morning—the first day
The torture I was told would make me better than many
It was all for my own good that beating and the abuse
I was reminded of the need to always respect those in power

They come for me at three in the morning—always
I stumble in the darkness of the thick foggy dream
I am a small boy again crying out for my mother
Silently I scream and feel the shame as I wet myself

They come for me at three in the morning—every night
I am weak I am scared and feel it must be all my fault
They beat me and I leave my body to escape the pain
As I awaken from tonight's post traumatic stress dream

Traumatised

What is the meaning of life?
If every night the past I do re-live
Not that sunrise brings any relief
In myself I have lost all belief

What reason do I have to live on?
If not to see my pain and anger avenged
On those whom my political views sowed fear
In me they saw a target for abuse and torture

What reason do I have to live on?
My worldly belongings they took away
I am but a pathetic figure as I go my way
Inside me a volcano awaits to erupt

What is the meaning of life?
In a world packed with flashbacks
I am on a daily diet of panic attacks
My life ended on the day of torture

What is the meaning of life?
When every heartbeat is driven by rage
In a life shattered to a thousand pieces
As I live my future an hour at a time
Is this the meaning of life?

Andrew Mutandwa

The Immigrant Nurse

In the mental institution that my country seems to be
The solution may not be political but mental health
Many fled the country to end up mental health nurses
Onward mental health soldiers, a job to do lies ahead
If all us immigrant nurses decide to return home

We will dispense much needed psychotherapy
To traumatised thousands roaming the country
And run anger management courses to a violent police force
We will assess aging politicians for severe personality disorder
And in our kindness provide them with dementia care

A Mother's Regret

I toss and turn in bed
As I struggle to go to sleep
One of my children is missing
It is a big house but the nest is empty

I toss and turn in bed
And wonder where I went wrong
I took a chance and left my home
A better chance to give my children

I fled from violence and torture
Fled too from economic demise and hunger
I work tirelessly long hard hours
Clothe, shelter and feed my brood

I toss and turn in bed
And know all cultural values are lost
As my child grows up all too quickly
Cushioned by child rights and human rights

I toss and turn in bed
As tears roll down and soak my pillow
Whose bed is my baby sleeping in tonight?
Will she be home tomorrow for her happy 15th

As I toss and turn in bed
Was it all worth the pain?
Flying half way across the world
To be alone and cry myself to sleep

Andrew Mutandwa

The Ugly Truth

Little Ruva is various shades of brown
She is a dusty little girl dressed in dirty rags
Her big head balances delicately on slender frame
She scans her surroundings not in hope but despair
She lives in a village which should be called 'Desolation'

Little Ruva is often called an ugly child
Only her mother, if alive, would remember her smile
Seven years it's been since Ruva smiled aged three
Her downcast big brown eyes hide pain and fear
She is a billboard those around her would rather not see

The ugly truth is little Ruva will always be ugly
Her face is permanently contorted by hunger and thirst
Arms and legs scratched and bruised as price for survival
Neighbours sometimes smack her then feed her leftovers
Gratefully little Ruva eats scraps and lives another day

Then it rains and washes away all the grime and dust
Little Ruva looks to the skies as if searching for her mum
For the briefest moment she relaxes and looks so beautiful
Another time, another world Ruva would play and smile
The little orphan girl might have been world's next top model
But little Ruva learnt early that poverty makes you ugly

[Ruva is a Zimbabwean name which means 'flower']

The Native

At what point do I change to be a new national
Ten years on I still think like the old national
I love to think and still dream in my native tongue
Surprise not that I seek only those who speak like me
We are bound together by a common unique accent
Easily picked out in supermarkets and nursing homes

At what point do I change to be a new national
Ten years on I struggle to be a new national
I still prefer my old dish of maize meal and beef
It brings back memories of glorious days gone by
Never mind that I do rely on cheap substitutes
As we buy treats with dodgy best-sell-by dates

At what point do I become a truly new national
Ten years on to Bletchley a monthly pilgrimage I make
Not to visit the historic town of world war code breakers
Still a town that draws together Zimbabweans in England
As we scramble to buy maize meal, beef and lacto milk
A meeting point for Zimbabweans craving the old life

Andrew Mutandwa

The Political Lesson

This big man has a wife sleeping alone and safely at home
He puts on his most menacing face as he trudges out of the door
The man is off to do his bit for ruling party and country

The two brothers have sisters they are very protective of
Their dad told them to always respect and protect all girls
Tonight they are Green Bombers, the party's youth troopers

Mary and Jane are the local daytime sweet girls next door
At night they are the band masters in the orchestra of terror
Jane and Mary believe everyone should support the president

The motley army of campaigners meet on a dark cloudy night
Onward towards a cluster of huts the army of thugs march
Even the dogs have learnt not to bark at the Green Bombers

Mary and Jane gather the villagers called the 'opposition'
They hold court and say these people have to learn a lesson
The females are singled out for a special night lecture and led away

Jane and Mary hold me down revelling in my pain and fright
I close my eyes as the big man has his way and ravages me
If it is punishment the worst comes from the two brothers

In the surrounding bushes the other women whimper in pain
As dawn approaches the party activists slink away like thieves
As they leave us we now know the danger of opposition politics

Quietly we return home bound by a dirty and painful secret
Not knowing which is the bigger worry HIV, pregnancy or both
Is rape a price ever worth paying for democracy?

Andrew Mutandwa

The jailing of Nigel 2008

What went through that little child's trusting mind
When the secret police crashed through the door
What did he think was happening in that commotion
When he and his parents were abducted and driven away

What went through the young mind of two-year old Nigel
As he languished in a Zimbabwean maximum security prison
What damage was done to the young mind of little Nigel?
In the 76 days that he was incarcerated in a dirty dingy cell

How desperate was the dictatorship to hold on to power
As they inflicted the ultimate torture to every loving parent
What went through the old deranged minds of his jailers
As they left their shift and went home to their own toddlers

What childhood memories will little Nigel have
Robbed of freedom and robbed of all his human rights
What amazing political power did toddler Nigel possess
That caused him to be incarcerated and denied toys

Diaspora Grief

Maria sits on the couch watching Home and Away
She takes in the pictures but her mind is far away
The girl is in a permanent state of grieving
Constantly shedding an invisible stream of tears

Maria grieves for the relatives who have died back home
She grieves for her favourite grandma and an older brother
She grieves too for the many funerals she never got to attend
Maria constantly sheds tears those around her do not see

Maria sits on the couch watching Home and Away
As she moans the life she left thousands of miles away
She grieves for the loss of security of her extended family
She grieves too for the loss of all her childhood friends

Maria grieves at being disengaged and alone in the diaspora
She finds solace in the abstract world of Face Book and live messenger
Her keyboard taps her way back into the lives of friends afar
As she browses photos and comments that melt diaspora grief

Epilogue

Portrait of a dictatorship

You have not lived through hell on earth until you have lived under a dictatorship, for there is no greater deposit of human evil than is epitomised by a life-time dictator as he presides over a thoroughly intimidated nation. Arguably, there is no worse dictator than one who starts off by being voted into office. His metamorphosis is sneaky, yet systematic and brutal. Initial excesses are accepted and forgiven because the people somehow feel a sense of gratitude for what they perceive as benefit of positive change brought about by his leadership—especially if the country has just emerged from a civil war. Such attitude only serves to strengthen the dictator's hand as he tightens the noose around his people.

To be strong, very strong, the dictator needs to surround himself with fiercely loyal flunkies and it is no accident that these flunkies do actually pick themselves. For, although many people think that in a dictatorship the first casualty is democracy, it is actually the economy and earning power. As an increasing number of people fall below the poverty line, the instinct to survive is triggered and different people react in different ways. As the number of jobs diminishes those of weaker resolve will gravitate towards the source of power to pick up the crumbs under the king's table.

Cabinet ministers are hardly ever changed no matter how incompetent they are. In fact, because such ministers know how incompetent they are, they will do all they can to ingratiate themselves to the dictator in order to hold on to their positions. A dictator has on a number of occasions been described as 'the son of God' or pointedly as 'Jesus' by a desperately fawning politician. Most, if not all the politicians in government are aware that if they should lose whatever post they hold they are unlikely to find a job in the open market of the private sector. Thus begins a vicious cycle of corruption, political thuggish behaviour, torture and arranged killings. However, once the politicians and or supporters of a dictator cross that line, they know there is no going back.

History has shown that in the past dictators have been executed once they leave office. An oppressed nation has also been known to take individual revenge on known cronies of a dictator. Unfortunately, this means a dictatorship will always be vulnerable and feel the need to perpetuate in order to survive. It can be argued that the International Human Rights Court at The Hague, far from being a deterrent, has forced many a dictator to strive to die in office.

There are two kinds of dictators—one uses brute force to subdue any opposition while the other bashes his people but is so good with words that he easily convinces the majority that this is all for their own good. As stated earlier, a dictator is never haphazard in his approach. He deals with his people in batches, targeting first of all certain key individuals, then a group of people, and to make his point ultimately clear he goes for a tribe and/or an ethnic group.

In the meantime, those not directly affected simply keep their heads down and hope they do not attract the attention of either the secret police or worse still, ruling party activists. However, there can be no hiding place from an all conquering dictator hungry for total domination. You either openly embrace his policies or you are deemed an enemy of the state. A dictator's freakish control permeates every corner of the country and every aspect of society.

This is perhaps epitomised in the most disturbing way by his tight control of the army, police and intelligence services. He carefully chooses the most fanatic members of the three organisations to lead and ensure he is fully protected. Those within the armed forces who attempt to show any dissent are made to quietly disappear, never to be seen again, or they have the regulatory fatal car accident.

Dictators love to see their own images everywhere which is why it is mandatory for every government office to display 'the portrait'. However, that in itself is not enough—one soldier must hold aloft 'the portrait' at passing out parades or other official marches, in a stark reminder of who exactly is in charge. Never mind that every little town has a street named after him.

The army, police and intelligence services are lethal weapons which a dictator ruthlessly employs to perpetuate his stay in office and this is displayed shamelessly when sham general elections are held. Opposition leaders are severely beaten up, ordinary members and supporters of the opposition are imprisoned without trial, and tortured—if they are lucky they will live. Otherwise they are simply beaten to death and quite often their bodies are never found.

A restless army can be a very bad thing for a dictator so in his sinisterly shrewd mind, he employs a clever but cruel diversion by turning soldiers into armed police to deal with real or perceived uprising even if that is in the form of a peaceful demonstration. The dictator's rationale is that if he keeps soldiers in barracks with nothing to do they will plot against him. Inside a dictatorship, an encounter with the police is a very painful experience, but those who have been dealt with by the army will tell you that is literally a brush with death. Having said that, the intelligence service, also often referred to as the secret police, is even more lethal. Only a very small number of people taken during the dark hours of the night by the secret police can live to tell their tale, unless mistakes are made and some witness raises a public alarm.

In Zimbabwe anyone carrying assault injuries will not be treated in hospital unless they first make a report to the police. Therefore, if the police have caused those injuries in the first place it means the victim will not be able to access hospital treatment. Those who can afford it seek the prohibitively expensive private treatment. Many victims of police brutality have since learnt that returning to report to the police, the same perpetrators of violence can be the most stupid if not dangerous thing to do.

In every country, a president or prime minister has a duty to appoint the most senior custodians of the law such as the attorney general and judges. In most cases such appointees conduct themselves with rarely questionable competence and admirable impartiality. However, in the hands of a dictator, these legal minds can be lethal tools of oppression. They will pursue those perceived to be 'anti-government' with the enthusiasm and assurances of a lion chasing a rabbit. At the same time, they will look away or drag their feet if there is need to prosecute thieves and murderers on ruling party or state sponsored assignments. The legal system in a dictatorship is like a gambling house which plays with loaded dice—only the house wins, all the time.

A dictator and his form of government can be likened to a boa constrictor as he steadily and relentlessly sucks the life out of his people. As a dictatorship unfolds, people start off by making allowances and adjusting to accommodate a harshly changing political environment. In time, they feel trapped and many simply resign to their fate.

A dictatorship impacts upon people in different ways and at different times. Therefore, a rather confused pattern emerges whereby while some people may appear to be coping, others will be facing death, torture, rape, or losing all their property in places strewn across the country. A mother gang-raped in the presence of her very frightened little boy is forever ravaged by post stress traumatic disorder. Several hundred miles away across the country, a farmer remains in a permanent state of bereavement, grieving for the loss of everything he worked for all his life, his land, his home, and the rest of his property—taken over by a smirking army colonel.

On the outskirts of the town, at a police station he will never be able to identify, an opposition politician pleads for his life as he is repeatedly tortured. Meanwhile, for most of the people some caricature of life, which they have come to accept as the new normalcy, goes on. My late grandfather, always said: "The resilience of the people of Africa comes from this weird ability to remain dignified under the most oppressive of circumstances". During his time, he only had to contend with colonialism before he was liberated and in his sunset years introduced to Marxism, socialism and the one-party state. Under the colonial government he was simply told he had no right to vote. Under the liberation government he was told he could vote but he soon found out that his vote was never counted and so made no difference to an election outcome—he thought this was more painful to bear. He died, still trusting the politicians, and still hoping one day things would change. I am still waiting too, grandpa.

A dictator can also have a soft side, well semi-soft, for lack of a better term. Yes, the hard man of politics can have a soft spot for women—the more powerful he is the more women he wants. The easiest way to meet his needs is to try and create a harem out of his pool of secretaries—'keeping it in the family'. Those in the inner circle of the dictator see his sexual dalliances as a sign of weakness and they either turn a blind eye or facilitate, for instance to ensure that the first lady remains ignorant of the goings on. As true as there is death and taxes, a dictator invariable ends up marrying a much younger woman as a shameless display of his virility, to go with his macho image. Sadly, even women who cry out for emancipation will abandon the wronged first lady and sing praises of a concubine.

Almost every African leader has had his share of wives as well as discreet and many not so discreet love affairs. Not to be included in the inglorious band of dictators, but worth noting, even the great Nelson Mandela went through three high profile marriages in his life—and age was never a barrier!

One of the most painful realities of living under a repressive dictatorship is that women are victimised more than men. Under a dictatorship everyone loses their human rights. However, when it comes to politically inspired brutality, men are beaten up and sometimes killed. For women it is arguably worse as not only are they beaten up, but they are quite often also gang-raped in the presence of their husbands or children. There is no recourse to justice.

What man would knowingly rape a woman who has just buried her child simply because she is a member of the opposition party? Only in Zimbabwe does this happen. This leaves many people wondering whether a South African-style truth and reconciliation initiative could ever work in Zimbabwe.

A dictator's sense of invincibility, arising from systemic brutality, often stretching over decades, can be so intimidating that it gradually turns a whole country into a nation of cowards. I use this term universally because even those closest to the dictator sit in his shadow so they can feel protected more from him than the outside world. General fear envelopes the nation. Many people are beaten up. Women are raped as punishment for opposing the dictator or simply not showing support for him. Cruelty knows no bounds as babies and toddlers are incarcerated in maximum security prisons together with their parents in an effort to inflict maximum pain. There follows a wanton rape of financial services and the economy in general driven by corruption at all levels of management, presided over by the dictator himself as he authorises farm invasions and business takeovers.

In the case of Zimbabwe, during the country's liberation war, Mugabe's combatants had a very inspiring song which was also a code of conduct which they were all expected to abide by. The song was titled 'Nzira dzemasoja' or, loosely translated, 'The Conduct of Soldiers' and it was meant to be a guide on what was expected of them in terms of good behaviour. It clearly warned the combatants against pillaging other peoples' property and said they must always pay for what they take. Such an anthem made them truly a peoples' army, respected by the people they were fighting for. It worked for a while until the commander-in-chief led his armed forces into an orgy of invading and taking over farms—and killing some of the owners in the process.

Under such circumstances, agriculture collapses and people starve. In the meantime, no self-respecting dictator will accept aid for his starving and disease-ravaged people as this is a sign of weakness—one cannot just give up 'hard won sovereignty' to cater for people who oppose the government anyway! It is anathema to a dictator's way to admit to failure. Inflation may be running at a thousand percent but a well-fed dictator will flippantly tell you the economy is set to pick up and, you guessed it, blame it on the machinations of some Western countries, with Germany, Britain, the United States and Australia leading the usual band of suspects.

No country in the period between 1990 and 2010 has seen infrastructure collapse in the way that Zimbabwe has crumbled. It has become a fractured country recognisable in very specific and grotesquely identifiable bits and pieces. First of all the country is divided into three parts, the urban, the rural villages and what used to be the commercial farming sector. The farming sector has virtually been obliterated to be replaced by some caricature of what in some aspects represent forms of medieval agricultural practices, characterised by slashing and burning and moving on. Those who wield political power have raped the land to claim ownership of what produce or livestock a farmer has and then move on for more conquests.

What chance does an ordinary farm owner stand if a high court judge decides to invade and take over his farm, supported by armed police or members of the army? To add insult to injury, there have been very cruel cases where the farmer, in an effort to recover his property, has had the case presided over by the very same judge or magistrate who looted the property in the first place. A lasting legacy of the farm invasion is not only the desertification of a once lush countryside, but a speedy emergence of a poverty-stricken nation of which 80 percent of the population is permanently malnourished.

Zimbabweans living in rural communities have gone through three different phases of control to the structure of their existence. Before the country was colonised by the British, villages where grouped mainly according to what chief they fell under as well as along tribal lines. Most of the chiefs, without any formal education were, however, blessed with excellent management skills in terms of planning the structures of their villages as well as apportioning land for cultivation and animal husbandry.

With colonisation, came more robust politicisation of village life with a central government that sought some detailed insight into how everyone lived and how that could be controlled. Much of this was viewed as sinister, including the positives, because most of the new policies and changes where never clearly explained and there was very little if any evidence of partnership between the government and the people.

Black nationalists seized upon this credibility gap to take advantage of a population that wasn't so much gullible but was desperate for change. The People were like putty in the hands of ruthless manipulators, also known as political commissars, trained and indoctrinated in Russia, China, North Korea, Romania and Cuba. The people were told they had their own destiny in their own hands and were deliriously happy as they voted for the first time at independence not knowing the dice was so loaded and that the storm clouds were gathering in the not too distant horizon. Such a scene had been played out in many other countries gaining independence from colonial rule, but many Zimbabweans felt that for them things would turn out gloriously different. Many analysts were counting on the fact that the majority of the nationalists were highly educated and that Zimbabwe boasted arguably the highest literacy rate in Africa. Of course recent history has shown how mistaken the ordinary citizen was—as he or she found themselves pushed into politically inspired brutality and unprecedented poverty.

Those bloody diamonds

The irony of the whole situation is that when Zimbabwe got very broke, the land, in its wisdom, chose a time when the people were at their most oppressed and poverty stricken to line up the pockets of a dictatorship by revealing hitherto hidden diamond fields.

Many people in Zimbabwe will always wonder what would have happened if those bloody diamonds had not been discovered in the eastern part of the country. The economy was down and out, with the Government printing and issuing mind-numbing but worthless billion dollar notes. Everyone in the poverty ravaged country had been turned into a millionaire, including illiterate villagers.

Many of a religious persuasion thought their prayers were about to be answered and that the dictatorship would soon collapse. However, further irony had yet to be played out. Some foraging villagers discovered diamonds. The army moved in and there was bloodshed. Suddenly, those in power had a defiant spring in their step and openly boasted "we are not going anywhere". The discovery and private mining of the diamonds by officials and supporters of Zimbabwe's President Mugabe signalled the death of the fragile and ludicrous government of national unity. Why would a group of *nouve* rich politicians, with a brimming war chest, be bothered to continue in a government of so-called national unity with a rag tag opposition whose members go to bed on empty stomachs almost every night? As the saying goes, 'The Gods must be very crazy'.

The Stockholm syndrome

In recent times ethnic cleansing and general killing of part of a population has become harder. Therefore, a good dictator will unleash such terror that half the population flees the country. The remaining people either support him or are too poor to find the means to run away or put up a fight. They resent being around, they resent being under the dictator and they resent the situation that has put the dictator in a corner. Strangely, some may actually start believing that it may after all not be the fault of the dictator that things have got so bad.

It is most ironic that a whole nation can behave like they have been kidnapped and held hostage for decades as a dictator presides over them. In the eyes of many of his 'hostage nationals' a dictator may actually start gaining some measure of respect and sympathy, although this may simply be some survival instinct kicking in. It is quite painful to hear some emaciated villager say: "He is not that bad". What chance does the villager stand if he is only fed vitriolic propaganda from government-controlled media while being denied any alternative views?

Hence, as he kills his people and loots the country, a dictator deflects attention away from himself by blaming it all on western countries and sometimes picking a fight with a superpower or two. It will always be a win-win situation for the dictator.

Nevertheless, a dictator doesn't always get things his way. This is very much evident in the raging battles fought in newspaper columns and more so in the anonymity of internet forums where it is always impossible to tell if a dictator's apologist or critic is at home or lost somewhere in the *diaspora*. Language used in these forums for and against is so putrid it breaks all journalism and publishing ethics as well as public decency. In a country where journalists are routinely beaten up and imprisoned, some nationals feel that this is the only way they can level the playing field against an equally determined and deeply biased state-embedded press.

For the average immigrant, life can be extremely challenging. Most people have to settle for jobs much inferior than their previous professions. Their lives are sometimes very isolative in communities that are often not very welcoming.

No matter how bad a dictator is, he is always guaranteed some cheerleaders, even during the worst of times. Not that there is such thing as a good dictator. Somehow, a dictator always seems to have apologists even from the most unlikely of people. Among the oppressed citizens, there are many who are prepared to cast aside their oppression if they think the dictator is being unfairly criticised by someone from a different tribe or race or a disliked foreign power. Therefore, many a valid point, argument or advice is discarded simply because it is coming from the wrong people, those deemed not belong. No one understands and employs the concept of divide and rule like a dictator. Quite often a dictator does not have to do or say anything as his people bash each other up even though he is the common denominator in all that violence.

Having said that, there are also, always, other usual suspects such as fellow dictators who somehow seem to feel there is safety in numbers. They will pontificate passionately about safeguarding their national sovereignty and even shamelessly talk about their own brand of democracy. It is no surprise, therefore, how dictators pick each other as friends and such personal 'friends' of the dictator are then foisted upon an unsuspecting people as a national friend, a hero of the people. Sometimes fellow dictators have streets named in each other's countries. Zimbabweans, for instance, were forced to embrace as friends of the nation, such despots as Nikolai Ceucescu, Kim il Sung, Muammar Gadaffi, Laurent Kabila, Laurent Gbagbo, and Mengistu Haile Mariam, to name but a few.

Dictators visit each other as a form of perverse therapy as they compare palaces and amassed wealth—oblivious to the plight of their emaciated people. It follows therefore that dictators also love shopping and have wives whose only mission in life is to go shopping. They scour diplomatic briefs for any conferences going on so they can attend or solicit for an official visit which is just another term for a paid holiday. It is a sight for sore eyes to see a dictator and his entourage foraging for bargains in some departmental store abroad—spending whatever little foreign currency the national reserve bank can surrender from its near empty coffers.

Making a diagnosis

Dictators seem to operate under a common and vicious code of practice in terms of how they subjugate their people and yet the world has never figured out how to erase this blight on society. It makes no difference whether that dictatorship is flourishing in Africa, Asia, South America or the Middle East. The madness of a dictator knows no bounds and yet, even in dictatorships, a country's constitution is usually very specific about how a leader can and should be removed from office by reason of insanity.

The challenge, however, is where to find someone brave enough to bell the cat. There can be no physician in the country crazy enough to certify an insane dictator. There are many who would argue that, although dictatorship is not included in the International Classification of Diseases, DSM-10 Classification of Mental Illnesses, it is certainly a very serious mental illness. Most dictators do show clear symptoms of a wide range of mental illnesses including personality disorder, bipolar, anxiety, depression and indeed schizophrenia.

A pervasive pattern of grandiosity, need for admiration, and a lack of empathy certainly fits the profile of one or two dictators I know. That is also known as a narcissist personality disorder as described in the Diagnostic and Statistical Manual of Mental Disorders, DSM-IV, Code 301.81.

A dictator is more than just a temporary inconvenience. People get killed. So many tragedies continue to be played out in Africa. In recent times, Ivory Coast has been a painfully shocking case study and reminder of how bad things can get. Thousands killed as the outcome of a disputed election result. The incumbent loses but declares he is not going anywhere any time soon. The opposition leader arms his followers and shoots his way into the presidential fortress. Other African leaders incapacitated and tainted by their own excesses and inadequacies, look on and pray they are not the next domino to fall.

Sounds familiar? Zimbabwe comes to mind. The world has become so insensitive that unless it is officially classified as genocide, the rape, torture and killing of several thousands of people is accepted as normal currency in any politically unstable country. No intervention necessary—not quite yet.

If and when a dictator is finally removed or, as is more likely, dies in office, he is invariably replaced by those who would have suffered greatly during his reign. The people should be forgiven for holding great hope that, as Sam Cooke sang, 'A change is gonna come'. Unfortunately, history is littered with replacement teams that have turned out to be a milder form of the same disease. Sadly, if not tragically, the people will have to settle for a contaminated democracy as the new players also look set to want to entrench and enrich themselves as reward for having fought to replace a dictator. They inherit a dictator's paranoia and view anyone else who is not a member of their political party, or dares to criticise their ways, with the same suspicion that was once reserved for them. After all, opposition politics often dies with the formation of this caricature called government of national unity. Zimbabwe's once badly beaten up opposition leader, Morgan Tsvangirayi, describing his relationship with long time ruler Robert Mugabe, was once quoted saying: "Over a long period of time you start to develop some chemistry."

Seeking Asylum

Ten thousand miles away, a young woman stands in court claiming political asylum. The Immigration Officer argues that the young woman claims that she was a member of the opposition party but she is unable to produce a membership card. In a democracy, the distinction between a member of a political party and a mere supporter is very clear. In a dictatorship it is a different story. The distinction is also clear—you either belong to the ruling party or you are an enemy of the state. Obviously all is lost in political translation.

The young woman is also unable to produce any medical records to prove that she received medical treatment following her alleged torture by the dictator's youth activists. The burden of truth is against the young woman. She starts to cry and the Adjudicator asks the Court Interpreter to calm her down. A few minutes later she indicates that she is ready to continue. Without warning she suddenly stands up and pulls off her cotton blouse to reveal a faded pink floral bra and a deeply lacerated body.

Speaking softly in her native tongue, the young woman says: "If I had gone into hospital, the police would have been notified and they would have taken me away. I cannot prove that I was raped by six men but what I know is that everyday I feel like I should have killed myself. I have nightmares every night. I tremble whenever any man looks at me and I feel dirty".

She pauses as she trembles slightly, and then continues in a voice that is getting progressively weaker.

"What is there to live for? My mother thought maybe things would be better for me here—I see she was wrong".

The young woman sits down and there follows a brief moment of very awkward and uncomfortable silence. The Immigration Officer puts her head in her hands and looks down at the papers strewn on the table. After a while she raises her head and looks at the young woman and silently mouths the words: "I am sorry".

The Adjudicator seems to take this cue and clears his voice. He addresses the young woman in a very heavy Scottish accent but with a gentle voice:

"You need to understand that there are tens of thousands of people trying to get into this country for all kinds of reasons, few of which I must say are genuine".

"Therefore, although generally the Home Office accepts that the situation in your country is very dangerous for some people, it is important that anyone claiming political refuge need to prove beyond reasonable doubt that their life was in danger".

"We are here to do a job and it is not an easy job. I am therefore, personally sorry that you have had to put yourself through this humiliation in order to give us the proof that this court requires. Unless the Immigration Officer has any further objections, I am granting you, with immediate effect, indefinite leave to remain in this country. You will receive confirmation of this ruling shortly, which you may also take to the nearest GP so that you can be given whatever medical support you require, including counselling,"

In their desperation, a significant number of people have employed all kinds of strategies or ruses in order to be granted asylum in foreign countries. Some have claimed to be victims of homophobic victimisation while others have feigned mental illness in order not to be deported back to their country of origin. Many have also simply disappeared into a black hole and live on a prayer hoping to survive each day as it comes and knowing they may never again visit home as they cling on to a long expired passport. It is a very lonely and stressful life—dreading every knock on the door.

Intoxicatingly Homesick

A man walks out of his favourite pub in north London. As he makes his way towards the Golders Green train station the mixture of alcohol and nostalgia overwhelms him and he starts to sing softly:

> *Beautiful Zimbabwe*
> *Beautiful Zimbabwe*
> *I shall never forget*
> *Beautiful Zimbabwe*
>
> *Rest in peace beautiful Zimbabwe*
> *Rest in peace beautiful Zimbabwe*
> *I will never see you again*
> *Beautiful Zimbabwe*

The man is angry with his country's leader. He is angry that he misses home, his friends and the rest of his family. He misses the mesmerising purple haze of the Jacaranda trees in full bloom. He misses too the intoxicatingly sweet smell of the rich red soil when the rains fall on a hot summer's day. He misses the food he grew up on—the junk food he now eats has turned him obese and he is now diabetic. He longs for his beautiful Zimbabwe—or his deceptive memory of what it used to be. He is intoxicated—but still homesick.

There are those who live in hope and regard living under a dictatorship as a temporary inconvenience. However, 30 years and counting, is more permanent than temporary. With a life expectancy of around 40, there is a whole generation of Zimbabweans who lived all their lives under one enduring dictatorship before they died of AIDS. There is a whole generation of five-year olds who have never seen a Zimbabwean coin as the country relies on a coinless US dollar economy. In some homes the world phenomenon called the Zimbabwean Billion Dollar note has been framed for posterity, either as a joke or a sad reminder of how not to run a national economy.

There are much older people who sadly remember days under another form of dictatorship presided over by colonial rebel Prime Minister Ian Douglas Smith, and actually feel nostalgic about that era. They each have their views on how and why the equally repressive Smith era was more palatable. As one old man sums it up, "With Smith we knew what we were getting, but the deception by these wolves in sheepskins has been a very painful betrayal by our own people".

Perhaps the most tragic commentary on life under a dictatorship is how grown men and women grovel for acknowledgement from a dictator—a fleeting smile, a handshake or a mere nod of the head will send a government official or a member of the public into delirium.

Cooking up a storm

Having said that, there is no greater ironic incongruity on the situation that Zimbabweans live under than the fact that as millions starve year after year, the country's leaders, including the President himself, are referred to as 'chef'. Any dictionary will tell you that a chef is a person who cooks professionally for other people. Although over time the term has come to describe any person who cooks for a living, traditionally it refers to a highly skilled professional who is proficient in all aspects of food preparation.

Pitifully, most of those calling out 'chef-chef' don't even get to pick up crumbs from under the tables of their well-fed, overweight leaders. So what exactly is this army of chefs, including 'chef-de-grande' himself, cooking for the famished—nothing but trouble? It all started during the liberation war . . . the war was won . . . and cult reverence created. While 'our friends' in North Korea have great and dear leaders, in Zimbabwe we are cooked up a political storm by our non-cooking chefs (aka *mashefu*).

At home abroad

Without exception, whatever their reasons for leaving the country, any Zimbabweans you come across do miss home and they miss their traditional foods. This is why many will travel up to 50 miles or longer to visit particular shops selling products from South Africa and Zimbabwe. We still cannot do without our specially cut beef, tripe (guru), cattle feet (mazondo) and 'boerwors' sausages. At such places as one in UK's town of Bletchley, up to a hundred 'Zimbos' can turn up on a Saturday morning to stock up on meat, maize meal, Mazoe drinks, cultured milk (lacto) and other seasonal treats such as white mealies and fresh nuts.

The internet is littered with clips of people demonstrating how to cook the national dish of 'sadza' for the benefit of those who left the country before acquiring the appropriate skills. It would appear that Zimbabwean immigrants, wherever they have ended up, are settling in for the long haul. It is not easy, nay desirable, for any immigrant to cut that unique umbilical cord that ties one to their country of origin. This is why the hundreds of thousands of people who have given up waiting for the temporary inconvenient political impasse to pass feel criminalised for having taken up citizenship in their adopted countries. In Africa only a handful of countries embrace dual citizenship.

Dictatorships tend to have a very long lifespan. This means that there are bound to be generations who may never have a reference point of democratic principles and good governance practice in their own mother country. A few lucky ones carry only a faded picture in their pocket hoping it will all turn out to be only a temporary inconvenience.

C'est la vie.